The Jane Austen Quiz and Puzzle Book

by
Maggie Lane

ABSON BOOKS

Abson Books   Abson   Wick   Bristol

To Julia

ABSON BOOKS, Abson, Wick, Bristol, England
First published in Great Britain, June 1982.

© Maggie Lane.
Design: Paul Lane. Typesetting: Gina Shepperd

ISBN 0 902920 48 0
Printed at the Burleigh Press, Bristol, England.

How to use and enjoy the Jane Austen Quiz and Puzzle Book

In the following pages you will find a variety of puzzles and quizzes designed to test your knowledge of the novels of Jane Austen. All the answers may be found in the six novels; the fragments and juvenilia have not been used.

The illustrations in this book are by Hugh Thomson and Charles Brock from the Macmillan edition of the novels published in the 1890's. As well as looking decorative, these drawings form a puzzle in themselves, since you are invited to guess which quotation formed the original caption to each one. To help you, the name of the novel to which it belongs is printed above each illustration, and the answers are given at the back of the book together with the answers to the crosswords, word search puzzles, name games and quizzes.

There is one crossword for each novel, all the clues being quotations from it. Similarly with the name games, there is a puzzle for each of the six novels. The idea here is to fit the names of the characters into the blank squares, reading across, and a further character will appear between the bold lines reading down. Only one proper name is used for each 'across' character - a full point denotes a title of some kind.

Many people will be familiar with word search puzzles, but for those to whom they are new, the object is to discover certain categories of words concealed in a grid of letters. These words may read horizontally, vertically or diagonally - backwards or forwards - and letters may be used more than once, or not at all. There are three word search puzzles inspired by Jane Austen's novels, with the themes of Country Homes, City Streets and Servants. In each case one name has been picked out to start you off; draw lines round the others as you find them, noting them also in a list on the page, so that you can later check them against the answers at the back.

Finally, thirteen quizzes challenge your memory of all aspects of Jane Austen's world: Weather, Food, Appearances, Towns, Clothes, Christmas, Names, Colours, Months, Relations, Houses, Occupations and London. I hope you will find both quizzes and puzzles enjoyable and satisfying to solve; and whether the answers spring readily to mind, or whether the search for some elusive reference gives you a happy excuse for a little rereading, I trust you will derive as much pleasure from this light-hearted but not irreverent approach to those six delightful novels as I did in compiling what follows.

M.L.

Emma

"   "

Weather

Who

1   Acquired a sun tan

2   Longed for a frost

3   Hoped for rain

4   Dreaded the possible heats of September

5   Recognised a puddle when he saw one

6   Kept her neighbour talking in the wind

7   Borrowed two umbrellas from a farmer

8   Enthused over an unclouded night sky

9   Was once snowed up at a friend's house for a week

10 Thought more wine should be drunk in a foggy climate

11 Deplored the effect of a sharp frost on female faces

12 Required his own skies and barometers about him before he would promise sunshine

Name Game 1

L O U I S A

Pride and Prejudice

" "

Northanger Abbey

" "

Across

1 and 3. Let other pens dwell on … and … (5,6).

5 About thirty years … , Miss Maria Ward, of Huntingdon (3).

8 '… is a black word' (5).

9 'How glad I am to see you so much in … !'(4).

11 'What an amazing match … her!' (3).

12 Her happiness on this occasion was very much à la … (6).

15 A girl so brought … must be adequately provided for (2).

17 He came home, not to stand and be talked to, but to … about and make a noise (3).

18 'Refuse Mr Crawford! Upon what … ?' (4).

19 'We put in the apricot against the stable wall, which is now grown such a … tree' (5).

20 'There is no end of the evil let loose upon … ' (2).

21 In all probability the last … on that stage (5).

23 … to her interests, and considerate of her feelings (4).

24 'But cousin - will it … to the post?' (2).

Down

1 'You must see the importance of getting in the … ' (5).

2 'That … gate, that ha-ha, give me a feeling of restraint' (4).

3 'You have been in a bad school for … in Hill Street' (9).

4 'I will not do her any harm, dear little … !' (4).

6 'How beautiful, how welcome, how wonderful the … !' (9).

7 'Fanny, ring the … ; I must have my dinner' (4)

10 'Then the point is clear. Miss Price is not … ' (3)

13 'Here's harmony! here's … !' (6).

14 'Cut down an … ! What a pity!' (6).

16 It was a very … wedding (6).

21 'I am not … fond of acting as I was at first' (2).

22 The ' … ' and the 'yes' had been very recently in alternation (2).

Food

1 What remnants of breakfast did William Price leave on his plate

2 Which three fruits were arranged in pyramids at Pemberley

3 Which two cheeses did Mr Elton eat with celery and beetroot

4 What did Dr Grant send back because it was too tough

5 What did Mr Woodhouse send back because it was not boiled enough

6 With which delicacies did Mrs Jennings try to console Marianne

7 What did Emma's nephews eat at Hartfield on 24th December

8 What did Willoughby eat and drink at Marlborough

9 What food was suggested for the picnic at Box Hill

10 Whilst Mary Crawford played the harp what was served

11 What type of soup did Mr Bingley promise at his ball

12 What gift did Mrs Martin make to Mrs Goddard

Sense and Sensibility

"   "

Country Homes
Word Search

The grid contains the names of 25 country homes from the novels of Jane Austen. The words 'Park', 'Abbey' etc. are not included. Encircle the answers on the grid and list them in the space below.

```
Y E C A L N O T N R O H T N H
E N M B R C O M B E M A G N A
L L E W N O D L E C L D M L L
R H V T O O P E L J R J E N L
E C E R H O T E L O M N Y O E
B N R S E E D R F A O M N R N
M Y I G U I R S E R F G L L H
E L N N Y P N F T L B O R A A
P L G I U U P H I O L P R N M
O E H S H E A E U E N U R D A
R K A O T N C R R H L A F R N
H L M R G O N T C E D E D S
T W A E D L E I F T R A H R F
N L R A N D A L L S D O A B I
I A A N R T L E B M O C S N E
W E T T E N O T R E H T O S L
N O T R A B C L E V E L A N D
```

Appearances

Who said of whom

1 "What a bloom of full health, and such a pretty height and size; such a firm and upright figure"

___

2 "Her face is too thin; her complexion has no brilliancy; and her features are not at all handsome"

___

3 "Such a charming man! So handsome! so tall!"

___

4 "A brown skin, with dark eyes, and rather dark hair"

___

5 "The last time I saw her she had a red nose, but I hope that may not happen every day"

___

6 "I never saw anything so outrée! - Those curls! - This must be a fancy of her own"

___

7 "Her hair arranged as neatly as it always is, and one little curl falling forward as she wrote"

___

8 "Such a nasty little freckled thing!"

___

9 "His figure is not striking; his eyes want all that spirit, that fire, which at once announce virtue and intelligence"

___

10 "Something so formal and arrangé in her air! and she sits so upright!"

___

11 "Who would have thought she could be so thin and small!"

___

12 "His face the colour of mahogany, rough and rugged to the last degree, all lines and wrinkles"

___

Mansfield Park

"   "

Name Game 2

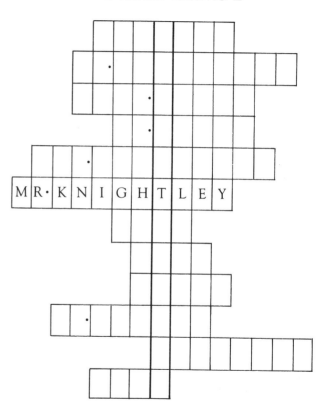

M R · K N I G H T L E Y

Persuasion

Across

1 "He is not so … as real gentlemen" (7)
4 "The first two dances of this little projected … " (4)
7 "How shall we ever recollect half the … for grandmama?" (6)
9 "My playing is no more like hers, than a … is to sunshine" (4)
11 The appearance of the little sitting room as they …, was tranquillity itself (7)
13 "… precious treasures" (4)
15 So much to ask and to say as to …, touch and pedal (4)
18 Not one left to bake … to boil (2)
20 "As long as so many … were sold, it did not signify who ate the remainder" (5)
22 "It will be an 'Exactly …' as he says himself" (2)
23 "Two things moderately clever, or … things very dull indeed" (5)
24 "A little …, vulgar being" (7)
25 "But I have never fixed on … or any other month" (4)

Down

1 "Nonsensical …!" was his reply (4)
2 "An … boiled very soft is not unwholesome" (3)
3 "Young … are delicate plants" (6)
4 "I shall wear a large bonnet, and bring one of my little … hanging on my arm" (7)
5 "I want her to … down upon the bed" (3)
6 "I … rather proud of little George" (2)
8 "Our part of London is so … to most others!" (8)
10 "And then fly off, through half a sentence, to her mother's old …" (9)
12 "These are the sights, Harriet, to … one good" (2)
14 "It was the dimensions of some famous …" (2)
16 "If she can hesitate as to 'Yes' she ought to say '…' directly" (2)
17 "Brother and …! no indeed!" (6)
19 "With his …, and his sheep, and his library, and all the parish to manage" (4)
20 "… too! Bless me!" (4)
21 "Here comes this dear old … of mine" (4)

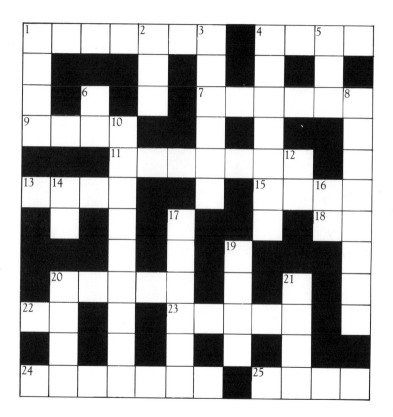

Towns

In which town did

1 Henry Crawford break his journey from Mansfield to Bath

2 Mr Shepherd attend the quarter-sessions

3 Colonel Forster make enquiries of the postilions

4 Isabella Thorpe eat ices at a pastry-cook's

5 The Musgrove daughters go to school

6 Georgiana Darcy consent to an elopement

7 Augusta Hawkins become engaged

8 Edward Ferrars learn of his release

9 The Crofts begin their married life

10 Admiral Crawford purchase a villa

11 Mrs Allen shop whilst living in the country

12 Mr Dixon save the life of Jane Fairfax

Emma

" "

Clothes

Who wore
1 A pink satin cloak

2 Lace-up half-boots

3 A gown with glossy spots

4 A greatcoat with innumerable capes

5 A muff

6 Thick leather gaiters

7 Sprigged muslin with blue trimmings

8 A night cap and powdering gown

9 Lace and pearls

10 Clogs

11 A flower in her hat

12 Brown velvet and blue satin

Mansfield Park

"   "

Name Game 3

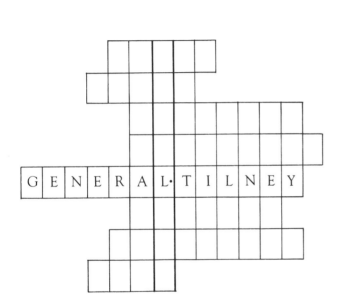

G E N E R A L · T I L N E Y

Sense and Sensibility

" "

Christmas

1 Which couple who later got engaged first met at Christmas

2 Who proposed marriage on Christmas Eve

3 To which house did Christmas bring 'a more than ordinary share of private balls and large dinners'

4 Where were tressels and trays laden with brawn and cold pies

5 With whom did William Price dine on 23rd December

6 How many were gathered at Randalls on Christmas Eve

7 With which family did Edmund pass Christmas week

8 And what was the name of the village in which they lived

9 From which Christmas duty did the snow keep Emma

10 Which fashion did Mrs Bennet hear of at Christmas

11 What kept the little Musgrove and Harville girls amused in the Christmas holidays

12 Whose acquaintance did Emma first make during a Christmas visit

Northanger Abbey

"   "

Across

1   "I must learn to ... being happier than I deserve" (5)

5   She was at the other end of the room, beautifying a ... (7)

8   "Songs and ..., all talk of women's fickleness" (8)

12 "In the name of heaven, who ... that old fellow?" (2)

14 "Rather a dressy man for his time ... life" (2)

15 The ... of knowing our own nothingness beyond our own circle (3)

17 "After taking privateers ... to be very entertaining" (6)

18 The last ... of the year upon the tawny leaves and withered hedges (6)

20 "A poor widow, barely able ... live, between thirty and forty" (2)

22 "You ... how it has carried away her freckles" (3)

24 "You have difficulties, and privations, and dangers enough to ... with" (8)

25 "Upon ... word, Miss Anne Elliot, you have the most extraordinary taste!" (2)

Down

1 "I have been to the theatre, and secured a … for tomorrow" (3)

2 "I would not venture … a horsepond in it" (4)

3 "No one so proper, so capable … Anne!„ (2)

4 Talked of poetry, the richness of the present … (3)

6 " … cousins in Laura Place" (3)

7 "So altered he should not have known … again" (3)

9 "Sits at her elbow, reading …, and whispering to her" (6)

10 "Rat-hunting all the morning, in my father's great … " (5)

11 "Journeys, London, servants, …, table - contractions and restrictions everywhere" (6)

13 To enjoy the … of a dead young lady (5)

16 Husbands and … generally understand when opposition will be in vain (5)

19 A dreadful multitude of … women in Bath (4)

21 "The … time that I ever fancied myself unwell" (4)

23 "All the happiness that a hazel … can be supposed capable of" (3)

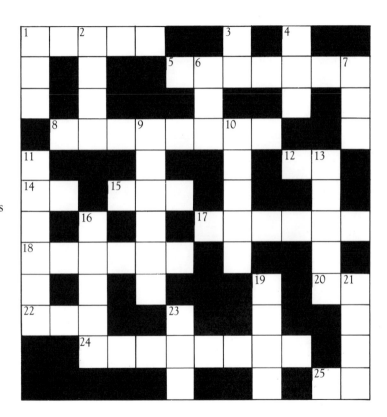

Names

What was the Christian name of

1   Mrs Clay

2   Mr Elton

3   Lady Stornaway

4   Captain Benwick

5   Miss Sharpe

6   Mr Bingley

7   Miss Bates

8   Mrs Forster

9   Mr Woodhouse

10 Mrs Suckling

11 The younger Miss Sneyd

12 Anne Thorpe's two friends

Pride and Prejudice

"   "

City Streets
Word Search

Contained in the grid are the names of 34 streets in the cities of London and Bath which are mentioned in Jane Austen's novels. The words 'Street', 'Square' etc. are omitted. Encircle the answers on the grid and list them in the space below.

```
B O N D H C R U H C E C A R G
A E B F R N E D M A C R X A R
K I R D Q U E E N O U W Y T O
E W J K R L R S M A C H D S S
R E I H E A T Y L B A T H A V
E S T M G L W K Q R B I C C E
T P I F P U E D G N I C R K N
S M U Q R O O Y E X J H E V O
E Y D W Z N L R E S R E V I R
H E N A E E W E O L I A O L O
C N O E H S V O N B R P N L D
N E C I D M T O D B L A A E R
A T L L K G I G I S K R H X O
M L X R B N A K A V N C A P F
Q U A S U L T R E T Z A O M D
U P O R T M A N S N E D L R E
M O S L I M K C I W S N U R B
```

Colours

What was the colour of
1 The curtains at Highbury Vicarage

2 The cushions at Sotherton Chapel

3 The counterpane at Northanger Abbey

4 The shawl preferred by Colonel Campbell

5 The ribbons on a hat in a Milsom Street shop

6 The Elliot livery cuffs and capes

7 Miss Andrews' sarsenet gown

8 Nancy Steele's hat ribbons

9 Eleanor Tilney's beads

10 Mr Bingley's coat

11 Catherine Morland's shoes

12 Mrs Elton's ridicule

Persuasion

"   "

Name Game 4

K	I	T	T	Y

Pride and Prejudice

"   "

Pride and Prejudice

"   "

Across

1 Her ... for ancient edifices was next in degree to her passion for Henry Tilney (7)
5 A neighbourhood of voluntary ... (5)
7 "I wish you could dance, my dear - I wish you could get a ..." (7)
10 "... men and women driving about the country in open carriages!" (5)
13 "What! always to be watched, in ... or by proxy!" (6)
16 "... honest relish of balls and plays, and every-day sights" (3)
18 "Were I mistress of the whole world, your brother would ... my only choice" (2)
21 "The quarrels of popes and ..., with wars and pestilences" (5)
23 "You really have done your hair in a more heavenly style than ..." (4)
24 "... is a vain coquette" (3)
26 "Do ... us turn back" (3)
27 "The difference of fortune ... be nothing to signify" (3)
28 "I have just learned to love a ... " (8)
29 "I will ... the Bath paper, and look over the arrivals" (3)

Down

1 The friends of his solitude, a large Newfoundland … and two or three terriers (5)

2 "Bath is a charming place, … " (3)

3 "…, candid, artless, guileless, with affections strong but simple" (4)

4 "I think … as beautiful as an angel" (3)

6 "I shall make but a … figure in your journal tomorrow" (4)

8 "I defy any man in England to make my horse go less than … miles an hour" (3)

9 "If there is … thing more than another my aversion, it is a patched-on bow" (3)

11 "How I hate the sight of an …!" (8)

12 "Wherever they are I will … after them" (2)

14 "My hair … on end the whole time" (4)

15 "…, these odious gigs!" (2)

17 "To hear you talk so much about the … bread at Northanger" (6)

19 "I gave but five shillings a yard for it, and a true Indian … " (6)

20 To attempt a … of her lover's profile (6)

22 Three … looking females (5)

25 "You know … is over head and ears in love with you" (2)

25

Months

In which month did
1   The Dashwood ladies move house

2   Mr Crawford visit Portsmouth

3   Elizabeth refuse Mr Darcy

4   Emma accept Mr Knightley

5   Charlotte Lucas marry

6   Jane Fairfax catch cold

7   Miss Harville die

8   Captain Benwick learn of her death

9   Mrs Palmer give birth

10 Edmund take orders

11 Fanny return to Mansfield

12 Emma first see the sea

Northanger Abbey

"   "

Name Game 5

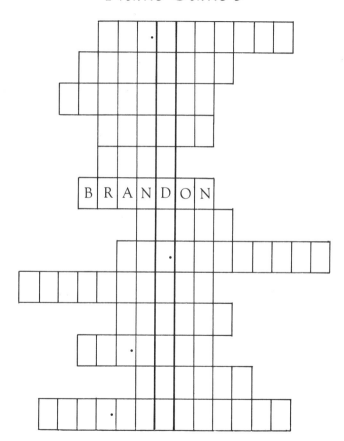

				.								

B R A N D O N

Emma

"   "

Mansfield Park

"   "

Across

1 and 25 "When a woman has five grown up …, she ought to give over thinking of her own …" (9, 6)

5 "I hope you saw her petticoat, six inches deep in …" (3)

6 "Happiness in marriage is entirely a matter of …" (6

8 "Her nose wants character; there is nothing marked in … lines" (3)

9 "Do not … on in that wild manner" (3)

11 "If there … but such another man for you!" (4)

12 "Stupid men are the only ones … knowing, after all" (5)

14 "I fancy she was wanted about the … pies" (5)

16 "I could have … scruple in abusing you to all your relations" (2)

17 "A little … bathing would set me up for ever" (3)

19 "I expected at least that the … were got into the garden" (4)

21 Set out to meet him accidentally in the … (4)

22 "I hope I never ridicule what is wise … good" (2)

23 "She is tolerable; but not handsome enough to tempt …" (2)

24 "… thousand a year, and very likely more!" (3)

25 See 1.

26 This … was to join in cutting off the entail (3)

1 "A most country town indifference to …" (7)
2 "They are … off together from Brighton" (4)
3 "If you are a good girl for the next ten years, I will take you to a … " (6)
4 So … a mixture of quick parts, sarcastic humour, reserve and caprice (3)
5 To be … of Pemberley might be something! (8)
7 The beautiful expression of her dark … (4)
10 "Follies and …, whims and inconsistencies" (8)
13 " … and earth! of what are you thinking!" (6)
15 "Where does discretion … and avarice begin?" (3)
18 A little ashamed of his aunt's … breeding (3)
19 " …, what is your age?" (4)
20 Secretly advising her father not to let her … (2)
23 "I have a very poor opinion of young … who live in Derbyshire" (3)
24 "What are men … rocks and mountains?" (2)

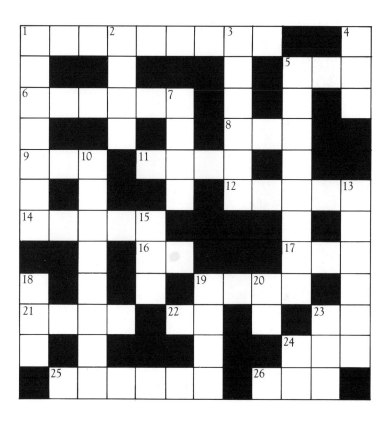

Relations

What was the Christian name of

1 Emma Woodhouse's grandmother

___

2 Fitzwilliam Darcy's mother

___

3 Catherine Morland's father

___

4 Edward Ferrars' uncle

___

5 Lady Catherine's husband

___

6 Mrs Smith's husband

___

7 Willoughby's wife

___

8 Captain Harville's sister

___

9 Captain Wentworth's brother

___

10 Lady Middleton's daughter

___

11 Mrs Fraser's step-daughter

___

12 Colonel Brandon's two cousins

___

Sense and Sensibility

"   "

Servants

Word Search

Concealed in the grid are 34 names of servants from the novels of Jane Austen. Answers may be either a Christian name or a surname, and 'Mrs' has been omitted. Encircle each name as you find it and list it in the space below.

```
V  A  S  I  L  L  E  I  Z  N  E  K  C  A  M
I  C  T  T  O  M  R  O  X  I  M  N  H  A  A
S  C  O  I  H  L  W  M  O  Y  P  F  I  V  D
E  E  S  R  A  G  K  P  C  J  R  L  L  T  D
L  B  M  L  N  O  I  A  L  X  L  Y  L  E  I
R  E  R  Y  N  O  D  R  I  I  H  A  R  A  S
A  R  E  K  A  T  I  H  W  E  H  M  P  S  O
H  E  F  W  H  G  H  K  S  T  E  P  H  E  N
C  Y  R  R  A  F  D  A  E  A  R  B  X  O  O
Y  N  O  I  R  A  L  E  L  N  M  A  P  T  S
L  O  B  G  R  L  U  M  V  I  D  I  C  A  K
E  L  E  H  Y  N  N  A  N  Y  C  W  M  F  C
D  D  R  T  P  T  H  O  M  A  S  E  G  E  A
D  S  T  U  L  M  T  N  O  J  S  E  M  A  J
A  E  C  H  A  P  M  A  N  U  R  W  D  Z  O
B  N  O  S  W  A  D  M  P  S  E  G  D  O  H
S  A  I  E  L  R  E  S  L  L  O  H  C  I  N
```

Houses

Name the house described

1 a new-built substantial stone house, with its semi-circular sweep and green gates

2 the garden sloping to the road, the house standing in it, the green pales and the laurel hedge

3 the broad, neat gravel-walk, which led between espalier apple trees to the front door

4 the mansion of the squire, with its high walls, great gates and old trees, substantial and unmodernised

5 the house itself was under the guardianship of the fir, the mountain-ash and the acacia

6 an indifferent house, standing low, and hemmed in by the barns and buildings of a farm-yard

7 as a cottage it was defective, for the building was regular, the roof was tiled, the window shutters were not painted green, nor were the walls covered with honeysuckles

8 its suitable, becoming, characteristic situation, low and sheltered - its ample gardens stretching down to meadows washed by a stream

9 the compact, tight parsonage, enclosed in its own neat garden, with a vine and a pear-tree trained round its casements

10 an old and not very good house, almost as close to the road as it could be

11 its viranda, French windows and other prettinesses

12 a large, handsome stone building, standing well on rising ground, and backed by a ridge of high woody hills

Pride and Prejudice

Occupations

What was the occupation of

1 Mr Palmer

2 Miss Lee

3 Mr Wingfield

4 Mrs Rooke

5 William Larkins

6 William Thorpe

7 William Coxe

8 Frederick Tilney

9 Miss Nash

10 Mrs Younge

11 Mr Darcy's great-uncle

12 Lord St Ives' father

Mansfield Park

"   "

Across

1 "He danced from eight o'clock to …, without once sitting down" (4)
3 "All I heard was only by listening at the …" (4)
5 "People always … for ever when there is any annuity to be paid them"
6 A ring, with a … of hair in the centre (5)
8 "I am excessively … of a cottage" (4)
10 "Sending them presents of … and game and so forth" (4)
11 "And such a mulbery tree in one … !" (6)
14 "He is such a charming …, that it is quite a pity he should be so grave and dull" (3)
15 "Don't we all know that … must be a match" (2)
16 The old gentleman died; his will was … (4)
17 "Your passion for dead … " (6)
19 "He admires as a … , not as a connoisseur" (5)
21 "The set of breakfast china is twice … handsome" (2)
23 "One shoulder of …, you know, drives another down" (6)
25 A driving … set full in their face (4)
26 "I love to be reminded of the past, Edward - whether it be melancholy or …" (3)

Down

1 No greater delight than in making a ... basket for a spoiled child

2 "You will be setting your cap at ... now" (3)

3 "In ... of your protegé you can even be saucy" (7)

4 "To give away half your fortune from your ... child" (3)

7 "Servilely copying such sentences as I was ashamed to put my name ..." (2)

9 "Lord! nothing seems to ... her any good" (2)

11 "We shall sit and gape at one another as dull as two ..." (4)

12 "I like a fine prospect, but not ... picturesque principles" (2)

13 "A very decent shot, and there is not a bolder ... in England" (5)

18 "In the ... Indies the climate is hot, and the mosquitoes are troublesome" (4)

19 Her visit was ... enough to detract something from their first admiration (4)

20 "Yes, I am ... drunk" (4)

21 "We will walk here ... least two hours" (2)

22 "Aches, cramps, rheumatism ... every species of ailment" (3)

24 "Men are very safe with ..., let them be ever so rich"

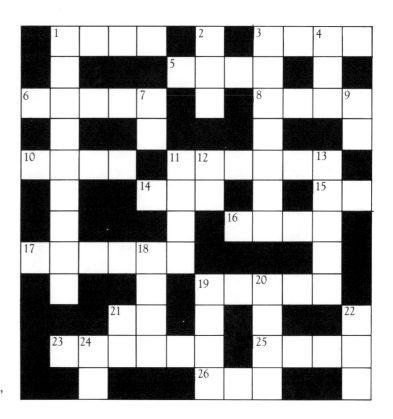

London

In London, who
1 Lived within sight of his warehouse

2 Exchanged some old-fashioned jewels of her mother's

3 Was courted with poetry

4 Declared Edmund to be one of the three handsomest men in town

5 Visited the dentist

6 Fought a duel

7 Purchased a pianoforte

8 Ordered a toothpick case

9 Resided in Putney

10 Wrote from Bartlett's Buildings by the two-penny post

11 Took Miss Steele to Kensington Gardens

12 Were seen together twice in the lobby of the House of Commons

Persuasion

"   "

Name Game 6

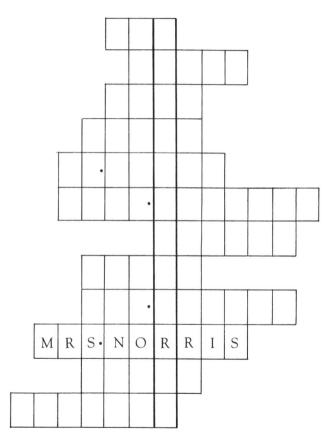

| M | R | S | • | N | O | R | R | I | S |

Sense and Sensibility

"   "

Answers

4 "'Who should come in but Elizabeth and her brother!'"
(Chapter 21)
WEATHER 1 Elizabeth Bennet. 2 Marianne Dashwood.
3 Mrs Bennet. 4 Anne Elliot. 5 Frank Churchill.
6 Miss de Burgh. 7 Mr Weston. 8 Fanny Price. 9 Mr Elton.
10 John Thorpe. 11 Sir Walter Elliot. 12 Mr Allen.

5 Sir Walter, Anne, Admiral Croft, Mary, Wentworth,
Mrs Musgrove, Louisa, Charles, Henrietta, Harville,
Mr Elliot. **(down)** Lady Russell.
"'No, no; stay where you are. You are charmingly
grouped.'" (Chapter 10)

6 "'Stop, stop, Mr Thorpe.'" (Chapter 11)

7 **(across)** 1 Guilt. 3 Misery. 5 Ago. 8 Never. 9 Love.
11 For. 12 Mortal. 15 Up. 17 Run. 18 Plea. 19 Noble.
20 Us. 21 Scene. 23 True. 24 Go. **(down)** 1 Grass.
2 Iron. 3 Matrimony. 4 Soul. 6 Evergreen. 7 Bell. 10 Out.
13 Repose. 14 Avenue. 16 Proper. 21 So. 22 No.

8 **FOOD** 1 Cold pork bones and mustard. 2 Grapes,
nectarines, peaches. 3 Stilton and North Wiltshire.
4 Pheasant. 5 Asparagus with a fricassee of sweetbreads.
6 Sweetmeats, olives, dried cherries, Constantia wine.
7 Roast mutton and rice pudding. 8 Cold beef and a pint
of porter. 9 Pigeon pie and cold lamb. 10 Sandwiches.
11 White soup. 12 A goose.
'So shy before company' (Chapter 4)

9 **COUNTRY HOMES (across)** Barton, Cleveland,
Combe Magna, Donwell, Enscombe, Hartfield, Randalls,
Sotherton, Thornton Lacey. **(down)** Allenham,
Everingham, Kellynch, Mansfield, Norland, Pemberley,
Rosings, Winthrop. **(diagonal)** Delaford, Fullerton,
Hunsford, Longbourn, Netherfield, Northanger,
Uppercross, Woodston.

10 **APPEARANCES** 1 Mrs Weston of Emma. 2 Caroline
Bingley of Elizabeth Bennet. 3 Mrs Bennet of Mr Darcy.
4 Catherine Morland of Henry Tilney. 5 Sir Walter Elliot
of Mary Musgrove. 6 Frank Churchill of Jane Fairfax.
7 Henry Crawford of Fanny Price. 8 Lydia Bennet of
Miss King. 9 Marianne Dashwood of Edward Ferrars.
10 Elizabeth Elliot of Lady Russell. 11 Maria Lucas of
Miss de Burgh. 12 Sir Walter Elliot of Admiral Baldwin.

11 'Busy at the pianoforte' (Chapter 11)
Harriet, Mr Woodhouse, Miss Bates, Mr Elton,
Mrs Churchill, Mr Knightley, Emma, Jane, Frank,
Mr Weston, Isabella, John. **(down)** Robert Martin.

12 'A gentleman politely drew back' (Chapter 12)

13 **(across)** 1 Genteel. 4 Ball. 7 Dishes. 9 Lamp. 11 Entered.
13 Most. 15 Tone. 18 Or. 20 Sacks. 22 So. 23 Three.
24 Upstart. 25 June. **(down)** 1 Girl. 2 Egg. 3 Ladies.
4 Baskets. 5 Lie. 6 Am. 8 Superior. 10 Petticoat. 12 Do.
14 Ox. 16 No. 17 Sister. 19 Farm. 20 Soup. 21 Beau.

14 **TOWNS** 1 Banbury. 2 Taunton. 3 Epsom. 4 Bristol.
5 Exeter. 6 Ramsgate. 7 Bath. 8 Oxford. 9 Yarmouth.
10 Richmond. 11 Salisbury. 12 Weymouth.
'He stopped to look in' (Chapter 24)

15 **CLOTHES** 1 Mr Rushworth. 2 Emma Woodhouse.
3 Fanny Price. 4 Henry Tilney. 5 Marianne Dashwood.
6 Mr Knightley. 7 Catherine Morland. 8 Mr Bennet.
9 Mrs Elton. 10 Mrs Allen. 11 Rebecca.
12 The portraits at Uppercross.
'Making her see how well it looked' (Chapter 26)

16 James, Henry, Isabella, Catherine, General Tilney,
Eleanor, Frederick, John. **(down)** Mrs Allen.
'They sang together' (Chapter 10)

17 **CHRISTMAS** 1 Isabella Thorpe and James Morland.
2 Mr Elton. 3 Barton Park. 4 Uppercross. 5 Admiral
Crawford. 6 Eight. 7 The Owens. 8 Lessingby. 9 Church-
going. 10 Long sleeves. 11 Silk and gold paper. 12 Baby
Emma Knightley.

18 'General Tilney was pacing the drawing-room' (Chapter 21)

19 **(across)** 1 Brook. 5 Nosegay. 8 Proverbs. 12 Is. 14 Of.
15 Art. 17 Enough. 18 Smiles. 20 To. 22 See. 24 Struggle.
25 My. **(down)** 1 Box. 2 Over. 3 As. 4 Age. 6 Our. 7 You.
9 Verses. 10 Barns. 11 Horses. 13 Sight. 16 Wives.
19 Ugly. 21 Only. 23. Nut.

20 **NAMES** 1 Penelope. 2 Philip. 3 Flora. 4 James.
5 Martha. 6 Charles. 7 Hetty. 8 Harriet. 9 Henry.

10 Selina. 11 Augusta. 12 Emily and Sophia.
'On the stairs were a troop of little boys and girls' (Chapter 27)

21 **CITY STREETS (across)** Bath, Bond, Brunswick,
Camden, Gracechurch, Milsom, Portman, Queen,
Rivers. **(down)** Baker, Bedford, Cheap, Conduit,
Grosvenor, Hanover, Manchester, Pulteney, Sackville.
(diagonal) Argyle, Berkeley, Brock, Drury, Edgars,
Edward, Gay, Harley, Hill, Lansdown, Laura,
Marlborough, Park, Union, Westgate, Wimpole.

22 **COLOURS** 1 Yellow. 2 Crimson. 3 White. 4 Olive.
5 Coquilicot. 6 Orange. 7 Puce. 8 Pink. 9 White.
10 Blue. 11 Black. 12 Purple and gold.
'Obliged to touch him before she could catch his notice'
(Chapter 18).

23 Bingley, Jane, Charlotte, Darcy, Georgiana, Mr Bennet,
Fitzwilliam, Mr Collins, Lady Catherine, Kitty, Elizabeth,
Lydia, Mary. **(down)** George Wickham.
'Love and eloquence' (Chapter 22)

24 'She stood several minutes before the picture, in earnest
contemplation' (Chapter 43)

25 **(across)** 1 Passion. 5 Spies. 7 Partner. 10 Young.
13 Person. 16 The. 18 Be. 21 Kings. 23 Ever. 24 She.
26 Let. 27 Can. 28 Hyacinth. 29 Get. **(down)** 1 Puppy.
2 Sir. 3 Open. 4 Her. 6 Poor. 8 Ten. 9 One. 11 Umbrella.
12 Go. 14 Standing. 15 Oh. 17 French. 19 Muslin.
20 Sketch. 22 Smart. 25 He.

26 **MONTHS** 1 September. 2 March. 3 April. 4 July.
5 January. 6 November. 7 June. 8 August. 9 February.
10 December. 11 May. 12 October.
'They all attended in the hall to see him mount' (Chapter 22)

27 Mrs Ferrars, Margaret, Marianne, Elinor, Lucy, Brandon,
Nancy, Mrs Jennings, Willoughby, Edward, Sir John,
Robert, Lady Middleton. **(down)** Fanny Dashwood.
'It passed to Mrs Cole, Mrs Perry, and Mrs Elton' (Chapter 53)

28 'William and Fanny were horror-struck at the idea'
(Chapter 37)

29 **(across)** 1 Daughters. 5 Mud. 6 Chance. 8 Its. 9 Run.
11 Were. 12 Worth. 14 Mince. 16 No. 17 Sea. 19 Pigs.
21 Lane. 22 Or. 23 Me. 24 Ten. 25 Beauty. 26 Son.
(down) 1 Decorum. 2 Gone. 3 Review. 4 Odd. 5 Mistress.
7 Eyes. 10 Nonsense. 13 Heaven. 15 End. 18 Ill. 19 Pray.
20 Go. 23 Men. 24 To.

30 **RELATIONS** 1 Catherine. 2 Anne. 3 Richard.
4 Robert. 5 Lewis. 6 Charles. 7 Sophia. 8 Fanny.
9 Edward. 10 Annamaria. 11 Margaret. 12 Eliza and Fanny.
'Introduced to Mrs Jennings' (Chapter 33)

31 **SERVANTS (across)** Chapman, Dawson, Ellis, Hodges,
James, Mackenzie, Nanny, Nicholls, Sarah, Serle,
Stephen, Thomas, Tom, Whitaker. **(down)** Baddely,
Charles, Hannah, Harry, Hill, Jackson, John, Maddison,
Rebecca, Reynolds, Robert, Wilcox, Wright. **(diagonal)**
Alice, Betty, Cartwright, Jemima, Patty, Sally, William.

32 **HOUSES** 1 Woodston. 2 Hunsford. 3 Abbey Mill Farm.
4 Uppercross House. 5 Cleveland. 6 Winthrop. 7 Barton
Cottage. 8 Donwell Abbey. 9 Uppercross Parsonage.
10 Highbury Vicarage. 11 Uppercross Cottage. 12 Pemberley.

33 '"Miss Bennet, I insist on being satisfied."' (Chapter 56)
OCCUPATIONS 1 Member of Parliament.
2 Governess. 3 Apocethary. 4 Nurse. 5 Farm Manager.
6 Sailor. 7 Lawyer. 8 Soldier. 9 Schoolteacher.
10 Lodging-house keeper. 11 Judge. 12 Curate.

34 'Sitting under trees with Fanny' (Chapter 48)

35 **(across)** 1 Four. 3 Door. 5 Live. 6 Plait. 8 Fond. 10 Fish.
11 Corner. 14 Man. 15 It. 16 Read. 17 Leaves. 19 Lover.
21 As. 23 Mutton. 25 Rain. 26 Gay. **(down)** 1 Filligree.
2 Him. 3 Defence. 4 Own. 7 To. 9 Do. 11 Cats. 12 On.
13 Rider. 18 East. 19 Long. 20 Very. 21 At. 22 And. 24 Us.

36 **LONDON** 1 Mr Gardiner. 2 Elinor Dashwood. 3 Jane
Bennet. 4 Mrs Fraser. 5 Harriet Smith. 6 Colonel
Brandon and Willoughby. 7 Frank Churchill. 8 Robert
Ferrars. 9 The Thorpes. 10 Lucy Steele. 11 The
Richardsons. 12 Sir Walter and Mr Elliot.
'Placed it before Anne' (Chapter 23)

37 Tom, Fanny, Mary, Julia, Dr Grant, Lady Bertram,
Edmund, Henry, Sir Thomas, Mrs Norris, Susan,
William. **(down)** Maria Bertram.
'"And see how the children go on"' (Chapter 46)

Front Cover. 'He stopped to look the question' (Emma Chapter 49)